Mare is a native of Guam, USA. She was born into a family of five siblings, her first friends. Playing school with her siblings cautions everyone that she had her mind on being a teacher at such a young age.

Mare's first venture away from Guam was to attend Viterbo College in La Crosse, Wisconsin. La Crosse is a college town known for its beautiful bluffs. Her teaching experiences began by working with elementary-age children in Guam and the states of North Carolina and Indiana. She taught in both Catholic and public-school settings. No matter where she is, Mare's passion and expertise in teaching was enjoyed by all for many wonderful years. Eventually, she went to the University of Arizona to pursue her studies in Second Language Teaching. Mare taught in Adult Education for almost twenty years. She did her lesson presentation of Crossroads Café-Indianpolis on TV to the new-English speaking population in Indianapolis.

Mare is now retired from her teaching profession and is enjoying on-going retirement with her husband in their home in Indianapolis. Mare writes her first book, *Transitions in My Life (Large Print Edition)*, and dreams to write more books in her senior years.

To all my dear nieces and nephews.

To Marilyn Salas, my maid of honour on my wedding day.

Mare

TRANSITIONS IN MY LIFE (LARGE PRINT EDITION)

AUSTIN MACAULEY PUBLISHERS

LONDON * CAMBRIDGE * NEW YORK * SHARJAH

A CIP catalogue record for this title is available from the British Library.

ISBN 9781035871162 (Paperback)
ISBN 9781035871179 (Hardback)
ISBN 9781035871186 (ePub e-book)

www.austinmacauley.com

First Published 2024
Austin Macauley Publishers Ltd®
1 Canada Square
Canary Wharf
London
E14 5AA

20240515

I am grateful to Sister Francis Jerome, RSM, my best English teacher. You were the first to recognise and to compliment my writing skills. I heeded to your advice to keep writing because my pen will take me to many places.

I am grateful to my husband, my soulmate, and love of my life. You have urged me tremendously from the beginning with your recommendations to write my story. You have tapped my talent, along with so much encouragement, inspiring me every day. I thank you for listening to the lines throughout my manuscript and for telling me everything sounds good.

I want to acknowledge all my Second Language Learners who arrived in my classroom so motivated with a desire to learn English. You all made teaching so much fun!

A Day in the Life of
a Chamorro Child (1953–1963)

I grew up in a very tiny village northwest of central Guam called Utan, Mongmong-Toto-Maite, where livelihood was quite remote. To get to our home you must go through two wild and steep winding roads which took you down to the valley where we lived. Only two houses stood there, a quonset hut and a two-storey home. Our church is situated right across from our home, but we can only go that route during the dry season. My brothers crossed the swamp to get to church to serve mass as altar boys, this was a shortcut! We otherwise took the longer route walking under the heat of the sun on these two steep roads. We passed bamboo trees which whistled with the winds while birds flew into the breadfruit and duduk trees. Some birds singing to their heart's content sat on the power lines that connected to a huge power plant in our village. My baby sister tirelessly rocked herself to sleep during her afternoon naps imitating the sounds of birds from her crib. Pak-a-doo were the baby words echoed by her. Banyan trees grew in the jungles around us. They were indigenous trees to Guam; ancient Chamorro spirits were thought to live in these trees. Such spirits protected the jungle! Never had any experience with the ghosts, however, it may be all just superstition.

In my village home, water was drawn from wells to do laundry. My brothers helped my mother draw buckets of water from the well till there was enough for my mom's use. It was hard work for my brothers to carry buckets of water along the hilly rocky roads that led back to my mom's work area. We enjoyed gathering around my mom as she did the laundry, my brothers climbed trees or ran around to play hide-and-seek in the swamps which surrounded the well. Mango trees and low-height coconut palm trees grew adjacent to the well. On the other hand, my mom was keeping an eye on us. She told my youngest brother to be careful climbing the trees. My brother responded, "Is it because if I fall, I may die, and I will not get married and have children?" When children live with security, they have faith in themselves and in those around them. They hope to emulate what is unfolding right before their eyes.

We also used rainwater which ran from our roof and drained into drums for drinking and cooking. My mother boiled this water to make it safe for our use. I find this well so memorable, in fact, on my husband's first visit to Guam, I took him to see this well. It was hard locating it as the well has met the land and of course, it is no longer in use. As we got older, my dad connected pipes from the well that led to our home, it became convenient to turn on the faucets where water flowed out. It was so incredible to get running water into our home!

Eventually, landowners claimed heirs to the land next to us and they started new developments. It was so exciting to have friends to play with and to have company walking to school. One neighbour would wake up her son as she saw us pass by her home on our way to school.

School sat on top of the second hill. You would immediately see yellow school buses which brought the local children, and grey school buses which transported the military children all parked in front of the school. Boys and girls ran into their classrooms as soon as they got off the bus. The military kids taught us that peanut butter and jelly made good box lunches. Quonset huts housed the students, and nobody realised how hot it was for that was all we ever knew. These rules stood out in our schools: no chewing gum, no attacking others with sharpened pencils, no throwing of rocks at each other, no running on campus, and no speaking of the Chamorro language. Once I arrived in my classroom, I would get a stomach-ache because school meant fear for me since I did not understand English. Obviously, teaching English as a second language was not yet researched. My big brother walked me back home and as soon as I got home my stomach-ache disappeared. This happened occasionally so my mom saw the need to have me transferred to the classroom of a local teacher who spoke Chamorro, my first language. Every day after lunchtime, my teacher placed us in a circle and my classmates demonstrated action words: running, walking, reading, eating, etc. I had to watch and listen carefully so I can understand what these actions stood for, from the demonstrations. Then, I was called to repeat the demonstration and identify what action it was. I learned English through this technique, "Total Physical Response," and of course in addition to classroom immersion all day, where observation and listening worked simultaneously. I was able to pick up the English language by the end of First Grade. Teachers in our schools were either local or military wives. The teachers from the U.S. Mainland always talked about how blue the sky and deep the Pacific Ocean were, and how green the island stood. So what colours were you expecting, a mind of a child may wonder. None of us was exposed to pollution of any kind like those found in big cities in the U.S. Our Stateside teachers told us about skyscrapers which were far beyond our imaginations. When Christmas came around, these teachers could not believe it was Christmas because it felt summerly and hot on any December day. My fifth-grade teacher packed an ice chest in her Volkswagen to chill her drinks. She treated all of us with ice cubes after recess time, a way to cool off from recess. Then, she had us number our papers from one to fifty and told us to list all fifty states and their capitals every day. That was how I memorised the states and their capitals for the rest of my life. In the beginning of the school year, we numbered our papers from one to forty-eight, by the second semester, we numbered our papers from one to fifty. Alaska and Hawaii became states the year I was in fifth grade. All subjects were taught by one teacher at the elementary level. Elementary classroom teachers taught all the basic subjects and gave us classes in fine arts and physical education. In art class, we made decorations for all U.S. holidays to decorate our classroom, no seasons in Guam but we had the holidays which arrive from one month to the next. Our teachers also taught us both traditional American songs and patriotic songs. I learned a lot about the United States from these songs. We had relay races and all kinds of outdoor games for our health and fitness. In the sixth grade, we had a very industrious teacher who motivated us to turn our classroom into a home. We sewed curtains for the windows and polished the floor with mahogany wax. Some students brought in half-cut coconut husks to shine the floor. The boys worked hard rubbing the coconut husks on the waxed floor to make it shiny. We were immensely proud of our classroom! It was till you got to the Junior High that there was departmentalised teaching. At that time, we were grouped into our classrooms according to one's level of academic performance. I remembered being assigned to advanced placement. My favourite class in Junior High was Spanish. I had the best teacher in the world who was a newlywed at the time. She invited us to her home to help prepare for our Spanish fiesta. Her home was in the military base, it was almost like leaving the island to go to another town to enter the base where she lived. Her home seemed like a castle to us with air conditioning and well-groomed landscaping. Up to this day, fifty-seven years later, we still send each other Christmas cards. We had talked on the phone prior to her first visit back to Guam. Her voice is still loud and clear as I remembered her. We have never crossed paths since those good old school days but hope to one day soon. It is quite unusual for a teacher and a student to stay in communication for such a duration of time, how I treasure this special long-distance and long-time relationship. When she returned from her trip, she called again. She enjoyed seeing all the changes in Guam, especially all the beautifully built museums which depict lots of history and culture. She found it so interesting that the Chamorro language is being taught in the schools. When I got to high school, my mom transferred me to an all-girls Catholic School. She was afraid I would get into boys and not focus on schoolwork. Obviously, I had a very sheltered life! The boys came down to our school anyways because we took the same buses to get home. I was not allowed to date. Surprisingly, I made it to the senior prom but with a chaperone, it was either I have a chaperone or not go at all. My mom asked her niece and her husband to be my chaperone. Then, my mom and her friend arranged for her son to be my date. Everybody looked so glamorously beautiful at the prom that I soon forgot about being ashamed that I had a chaperone that night. We were all so elated to see each other in the Blue Room of the Hilton Hotel. Had a great time dancing that night!

Every day when we came home from school, Mom was there to welcome us to a hearty meal. Then, there were chores to do. Homework came next, we used lights run by a generator to read and write. Mom was always beside me helping me read. Unlike my brothers, I was having a difficult time grasping the English language.

Most families have four to eight children, the father worked while the mother is a stay-at-home mom. In every household, sons and daughters were given chores that merely involved assisting parents with the tasks around the home. Daughters looked after siblings and did housecleaning. Since age seven, I was a full-time babysitter for my two youngest siblings. I changed their diapers and I often pricked them with the safety pins. My mom asked me why they were crying, and I did not remember that I ever answered her. I was just too young to use safety pins! My mother did all the cooking and laundry, and the rest of the household responsibility became mine. Having six children was challenging for her, I assumed. I have no children, no grands, no dogs, or cats to fully grasp this situation. In our adulthood, my sister would tell me, that I went into the convent because I already had my share of being a homemaker. My brothers' chores included picking papayas and breadfruit for feed, husking and grinding coconuts for the chickens and the pigs. While our father was at work, they worked on the ranch feeding chickens and pigs as well as grazing cows. My father had a cattle ranch which kept my brothers busy. A large area of the property was fenced with barbed wire to keep the cows in. As pasture had been eaten, cows were transferred to other areas inside the fence where there was more grass and forage for their feed. There were thirteen grown cows and numerous calves. Some are milking cows, so we did have a supply of fresh milk for the family. On some weekends, chores included butchering pigs or cows by my father, my brothers and men from extended families. Women prepared boiling water as part of the preparation. I remembered covering my ears because I could not stand hearing the wailing cries of pigs and cows as they were laid to the slaughter. Some meat was left to dry on the rooftops, while some were cooked immediately, and still, some were taken to the ice plant for storage. Others were sterilised with Clorox in boiling water, and it seemed forever to rinse them till it was safe to eat. At the end of the day, meat was divided among relatives who helped with the slaughtering.

Once children's chores were done, brothers and sisters played with the neighbours in the village. Boys and girls enjoyed games such as hide and seek, playing chase up on trees, jacks, softball, volleyball, Dutch ball, marbles, hopscotch, tether ball, jump rope, and red rover. The trees in the jungle had amazingly huge, wide roots, children can climb and race on them. Sometimes the boys went into the jungle to look for coconut crabs. Alongside the roots of coconuts, they saw mushrooms glowing in the dark jungle. They also enjoyed looking for Y-shaped tree branches to make sling shots. These sling shots were popular fun gadgets for play, so amazing because the boys made them. The boys used them to shoot all sorts of targets. Sometimes, they hunted birds like ko'ko (the Guam quail) or Sali (Micronesian Sterling). Once there was an abundance of these birds, it became a good meal called estufao which mom cooked in vinegar, soy sauce, onions, and garlic. In addition, big birds were aimed at just for fun so the boys could sharpen their skills or compete on who could catch the most birds. Boys and girls played together, but occasionally, little girls caught butterflies, grasshoppers, or praying mantes and put them in glass jars for show and tell at school. They also enjoyed playing with paper dolls. Other playtimes included playing school. I was always the teacher, we used surplus books that were given to us by our classroom teachers at school. Everybody listened to me, but their attention span did not last too long, they slowly walked out of my class and the game of playing school was all over. Other forms of child play involved picking fruits from trees. There were many tropical fruit varieties: papayas, mangoes, guavas, pomegranates, ates (sweetsop), star apples, pickles, iba (gooseberries), tangerines, oranges and camachili. Dripping with sweat on our brows, we sat down under the trees to find shade so that we could share all these fruits as part of our playtime. Everything was safe to play back in the days. There is a huge tree called the duduk tree where we picked jutos (nuts) from the ground, we had a contest on whose container will be filled first. The problem with picking the jutos was the swarm of mosquitos that lived under these trees. Our skins were all wilted from mosquito bites by the time we finished picking up the jutos. While this may be true, these mosquitoes did not stop us from the fun task. Mom rubbed dial soap to stop the itch. Our mother will boil these nuts for our snacks. We shared them with relatives and with the neighbours because we always had so much. It was nice seeing everybody enjoy them. Nobody else had access to a duduk tree! The land we lived on had everything growing on it. It sure was the land of plenty because every local fruit grew there!

When mothers finished their domestic responsibilities, they were usually outdoors chatting with other moms till it was time to make dinner before their husbands came home from work. There was a closely-knit village gathering in the early evenings. Novenas and rosaries were prayed at the end of the day in every home. The family that prayed together stayed together! On Sundays, everybody went to church, and two days a week, catechism classes were held at the village church after regular school hours. Mothers gave their children a nickel or a dime to stop by the small general village store for candies after catechism class which is a big treat for all children. How we looked forward to those days in catechism. On regular weekends, aunts and uncles came around to visit our home. Their visit was entertainment for us. They usually brought treats like chewing gum or life saver candies and I remembered how we would jump up and down in excitement as they arrived. Sometimes they would drive us to the Dairy Queen. Another uncle who worked in the schools was a maintenance guy, he handed us coins to buy ourselves ice cream cones or candies at the end of the school day. These were not extraordinary gestures by relatives but remained fond memories. Such were the simple joys of childhood living in Guam! Lots of generous relatives in our family. On other weekends, my family visited our aunts and uncles who lived along the beaches of Tumon Bay where my mom's family inherited land there. In Guam, it was common to have properties passed on to families down to the generations. While she visited with my aunt and uncle and did the laundry, my brothers and I will visit all the other surrounding relatives in the Tumon Bay area. We found fishing nets hanging everywhere, my uncle proudly showed us the fish caught the night before. I remembered how my retired navy uncle always had bacon in the freezer and many other fine groceries because he had privileges at the military commissary. We had bacon and eggs for breakfast when we went to his home. At the other houses, we were given only Japanese biscuits or toasts with butter or jelly. As a child, you learned that everybody's kitchen was different! He also served a fish luncheon. Later in the day, we headed to the beach and collected clams, challenging each other on who will find the most clams. We gathered the clams and took them home to be cooked. There were shells to pick along the seashore too and we took these back home to proudly show our neighbours or classmates at school the next day. Most children went to the beach to swim, but for us, it was more to explore the adventures of the seashore. A weekend to visit relatives at Tumon Bay was always an eventful day. Everything in my childhood days centred around families and relatives eating, playing, captivating each other in conversations and telling each other jokes. Once my uncle got hot charcoals from the open fire where my mother cooked food and dared my brothers to step on them. It was meant to be a joke, yet my mother did not appreciate it. Another time, my uncle had my two brothers in a boxing match, whose side was he on, I sure did not remember. He just wanted to laugh, but I bet he would not have laughed if it was a real fight. So much humour is typical or lets me add lots of interactive joyful play.

My father started building our concrete home from one pay day to the next. Every pay day he bought a truck load of cement blocks and stacked them up to begin the walls. All this hard work was done by my father and relatives who assisted him every weekend till the house was completed. It was a family affair! My mother prepared meals for all these wonderful builders. These relatives were skilled construction workers, carpenters, and painters. When it came time to do the roof, my father hired help from men from the Philippines who were very hard-working skilled workers too.

As years went by, my father had a vision to increase the scope of the land size by doing a landfill. He had a bulldozer clear and level up the land to fill up the swamps so that there was more land to live on. It turned out to be a magnificent transformation of what was once a remote village. This project of course took away lots of fruit trees, other plants native to the land, and much of wildlife. It was disappointing because we lost our jungle play areas as kids. However, my father had long-range planning, he knew that eventually, more people would move to our village neighbourhood. The utility departments installed water and electricity. My dad had more houses built on the land and did rental properties for our extra source of income. We started to have more new neighbours, some military families while others were businesspeople or still, other tenants were those who worked with Nasa. We visited each other's homes so there was a lot of socialising. We did not have to call each other on the phone to make appointments because it was "free" island-style living. Everybody's doors welcome visitors any time of the day. They were from the United States and we called them haoles, a nickname for Americans for both Guam and Hawaii. We had a good grasp of American culture from them in addition to what we were already learning from our teachers and military classmates in school.

Events like village fiestas, weddings, baptisms, and funerals were occasions when cows and pigs were butchered for food at the festive tables for all these social functions. For a village fiesta, the village people honoured the patron saint of their village by having a mass with a nine-day novena which is prayed in anticipation of the feast day. There is a procession with the statue of the patron saint on a decorated float that went in the procession around the village on the final day of the novena. The village people opened their homes to welcome people to a big festive meal after the procession. Every village throughout the island has its own patron saint. The celebrations were held every month according to the Saints' calendar.

During courtship, prior to the marriage, the parents of the boyfriend "nobio" meaning boyfriend visited the home of the "nobia" meaning girlfriend asking for permission from the girlfriend's parents for their son to marry their daughter. Months of planning for the "fandango", meaning the wedding reception took place soon after. Leaves from coconut palm trees and local flowers like hibiscus, plumerias, bougainvillaea, and orchids decorated the newly built tents for the fandango. A fandango began with a reception given by the groom's family Friday night before the wedding day on Saturday. The groom's sister presented the bridal bouquet to the bride, and his family also brought beverages for the big wedding to the bride's family. There were usually song presentations for the bride, and this became a delightful night, a band played, and dancing took place. At every traditional wedding, fifty per cent of the food came from the godparents. The groom's godparents provided fifty per cent of the wedding meal, while the bride's godparents donated fifty per cent of all the pastries. On the day of the wedding, after the church ceremony, a reception is held at the bride's home. Everyone took part in a wholly wonderful brunch. The bride and groom opened the wedding floor for dancing as soon as all the guests finished eating. Dancing followed and the wedding party ended when the bride and groom cut their wedding cake. They passed the cake to each of their guests and greeted all the guests one by one. It is a tradition that nobody went home till they got a piece of the wedding cake personally from the bride and groom. It was wrapped in a beautiful wedding napkin with the bride and groom's name and the date of the wedding. The wedding cake was a gift from the godparents of the bride and groom.

For a Christening, all babies were baptised with a saint's name or names of favourite relatives. Celebration is held on a Sunday immediately following the baby's Baptism at the church. Close relatives and friends were all invited to this celebration. It is a tradition for the baby's godparents to purchase the baptismal gown and to contribute a big sum of money to their godchild. The godparents also take responsibility for the child's Christian upbringing should the parents not be able to do so. It was a custom for Godparents to stay connected to their godchildren up to the time they get married.

At a time when there is death in the family, a nine-day rosary is prayed immediately after one's death. All relatives and friends of the deceased attend this ritual. Refreshments prepared by different family members were served every evening after the rosary. This is a social evening to bring cheer and support to the grieving family. On the day before the funeral, a wake is held, and a meal was prepared to serve all the people who attended. All the in-laws do the food preparations! At every ritual, there is always food galore served as a gesture of appreciation for all the people who were in attendance. Families and close friends helped the family with this special meal since several hundred relatives and friends came to pay their respects. For those who do not offer food to assist the grieving family, an envelope filled with cash was given instead. At the funeral, a donation box is placed next to the coffin for all to make their monetary offerings. The donated money can be used to pay for the meal that was served or to help pay with the funeral expenses. In Guam everyone seems to be related to each other, everyone knew everybody so wakes and funerals are well-attended on this tiny island. The following year, the first death anniversary of loved ones is observed, and once again the death ritual is revisited.

After World War II, one of Guam's leaders suggested that we celebrate Guam's liberation from the Japanese. The U.S. military leaders agreed to commemorate this important event. To this day, this Liberation Day continues to be celebrated every July 21st. There are festivities which include a queen contest, a month-long summer carnival with food, games, rides, refreshments, and a mile-long parade with thousands of floats, and marching bands by both local and military groups and by the different village schools. It was an exciting event for the whole family. I remembered going home with prizes I won from the games and there is a special plastic doll that my dad bought me every year at this carnival.

The three most important church events are Christmas, Easter, and the Feast of the Immaculate Conception. At Christmastime, a nine-day novena is prayed in family homes. A Nativity scene made of moss is set up in the living room which took the place of the Christmas Tree for some families. The focus of Christmas is the birthday of the Christ Child, better known as Nino. Each family chose whether their novenas would end on Christmas Eve, Christmas Day, New Year's Eve, New Year's Day, or on the Feast of the Magi. These novenas are long-standing traditions that were passed on from mother to daughter. One lady called "techa" is chosen to lead the novena. On the ninth day, a festive celebration is held.

The novena leader is gifted with food such as pastries, roast pig, and anything from the festive meal to take to her family as a stipend for having led the nine-day novena prayers. My mother was a well-known techa. How we looked forward to bags of delicious festive food she would bring to our home. On Christmas Day, the altar boys and the members of the church choir visited all homes for Christmas carolling throughout the village. One of the altar boys carried a statue of the Infant Jesus while another altar boy carried a donation box from house to house. All the families stopped their Christmas parties to venerate the Infant Jesus when He is brought to their door. This is a very moving moment for all families! Each family paused to acknowledge the meaning of Christmas with much adoration. Families give a donation to the Christ Child whose birthday was being celebrated. Families served refreshments to the carolers who visited shortly before they started moving on to the next house. The choir and the altar boys continued with their Christmas carolling till all homes were reached on Christmas Day. For Holy Week, children did not go to school, nor were they allowed to play or make any kind of noise to observe the Passion. Children were told that a Lenten pig, "babueng Kuarisma" will haunt us down if we misbehave. A funeral procession of the Crucified Christ all decked with white and purple flowers in a coffin is held on Good Friday. At the Good Friday services, people lined up to venerate the crucified Christ. Everybody went to church for the Easter Tridium. Children were so happy on Easter Sunday that for now they could run, jump, and play together and make all the noise they can make. They also knew a big dinner is served for the whole family on Easter Day. Both Christmas and Easter were times for families to come together. This is possible since everybody lived nearby, no need for big travelling because they all lived only a short distance away from each other.

The Feast of the Immaculate Conception was held on December 8th which is celebrated by the thousands with a mass and followed by a solemn island-wide procession around the capital to honour Santa Marian Kamalen who stood in a decorated float highlighting this event. In the procession, she is led by children dressed as angels and archangels, little maids all dressed in blue formal gowns with a tiara on their heads, and children all dressed in their First Communion clothes. This is a special day for children because this is the day, they made their First Communion. All religious organizations from the different parishes throughout the island lined up for this religious event and a fiesta meal is served after the ceremony.

There were no shopping malls, clothes were bought from department stores that served the island owned by local people: Tendan Nene, Town House, The Emporium, Marianas Sales, and The Department Store. Some mothers shopped for clothes from J.C. Penny, Montgomery Ward, or Sears catalogues. It was always exciting when the orders arrived. There were only three supermarkets on the whole island: Torres', Ada's and Bilmar Grocery Stores. There were many tiny general stores which had staple food items and household goods. They also sold beer and were a hub for some fathers who stopped there after work to relax from the hard day's work before heading home to be with their families for dinnertime. There was one ice plant that sold ice to families. Our refrigerators did not make ice, ice was purchased after every grocery shopping to chill all the foods. There were family-owned restaurants, but very few. Jo and Flo's was a Mexican Restaurant with fine dining and there was Jeff's Pirate's Cove situated along the beach which had local favourites. There was one bar in the capital city, "Hagatna", but the general stores were more common places for men to stop by for a bottle of beer.

It is important to mention the use of names for people in Guam. At Baptism, a baby is given a Saints' name or the name of the best relative for their first name. However, to keep track of which family surname one is referring to, we have a "better known as" system attached to our surnames. "Better known as" is usually derived from what the family is known for. My family is "better known as" Madoya because my grandmother made a living selling banana fritters called madoya all her life and that is what is known about our Duenas family. The "better known as" is affixed to your last name according to the craft, service, or pastime of your ancestors. This "better known as" system is commonly used for obituaries and announcements. For example, when I die, my death announcement will say Mare Duenas-Hewlett "better known as Madoza". Sometimes when people are speaking in conversation and there is a need to clarify which family one is speaking about, "better known as" became necessary.

A super typhoon called Karen in 1962 devastated the whole island. It was the most powerful tropical cyclone to hit Guam. It has been known to be the most destructive in the island's history with a disastrous fury that swept across the island at 200 mph winds. I remembered the howling sounds of the winds as they swung trees and attempted to tear off the roofs. A bolt of intense lightning flashed and along came with it rumbling sounds of thunder. It was a scary night as we just held each other arm in arm and prayed. Once our roof got blown away, rains poured in. My mom

25

saw water coming in and panicked, she thought that the waters from the swamps had risen to bring flood into our home. My dad told her, no we just lost part of our roof. We lived in a concrete home that had a tin roof which can easily get blown off by heavy gusts of wind. For people who lost their entire homes, they lived in tents for a long time. Salvation Army and the Red Cross helped the islanders. Schools went in double sessions. No matter the hardship, everybody was just grateful to God that we were safe. Post typhoon days were fun for all children, schools were closed, and no electricity meant lots of family time in shared conversations and outdoor fun by an open fire. We went outside to look at the fallen trees, gazed at how the massive land had been swept cleaned and we saw the other side of the village with all the debris from afar. Men worked hard at clearing the land from the debris. We picked coconuts, some still young and green, and others brown and ready for cooking. We poked an opening on one side of the coconut to drink the juice, then we opened them with machetes and scooped the white meat to eat and enjoy. Our dad built a fire over a half drum filled with sand so mom can cook all our meals. It was an opportune time for our dad to tell us stories about the Japanese occupation in Guam. We hardly had Dad home for he was always at work. He shared an incident with a Japanese soldier. He hid under a bed and hugged the statue of his patron saint, St. Ignatius when he saw him coming. When this Japanese soldier swung a machete under his bed it just escaped him. How thankful he felt! My mom usually told us stories about how they rode on the carabao to get from one end of the island to the other end. Her stories told of an island paradise in Guam when she was a child before the war. She talked of the peacefulness of the island and its people before World War II. After Typhoon Karen, it was time to rebuild the whole island and bring about change. Island-wide reconstruction took place, the building of concrete homes for residential homes, schools, and offices were in demand. The devastation for further typhoons were not as bad thereafter since concrete homes and buildings were built to withstand any massive typhoon. The only thing that one must do to prepare for typhoons is stock up on food, get batteries for flashlights, check if generators worked, store water in containers, and put-up shutters on glass windows. People who were less fortunate and do not have concrete homes will pack food, pillows and blankets to find shelter in the public school buildings or in power plants. These were momentous times, however, it seemed like a picnic time since many families visited each other and the children all played together in these shelters. Everybody seemed to ignore the fact that there was a typhoon going on. People were very friendly to each other and everything looked like party time. It was quite interesting how everybody would take out the food they have packed to share with each other. Families were very generous to each other! Eating is a favourite time, oh how we love to eat! Eating is entertainment!

My Mother's Plea

Motherhood is a gift to most women! Every mother will plea for help from God when the child from her womb enters the world with illness or with special needs. Thirty-three days after I was born, I was sick with pneumonia and whooping cough. My mom sought Divine Intervention. Like what most Catholic mothers would do, petitioning to Our Blessed Mother through Jesus her son became her constant prayer. As a little girl growing up, conversations always gave way to my mother's promise to give me back to God if I got well. Every visitor who came to our home heard about my mom's promise to God. She spoke of hospital instruments like tall needles and oxygen tanks that were guided by God's hands working in me to give me a quality of life. Relatives who visited me in the hospital told me about how I indescribably drank so much milk which gave them so much hope. They declared this baby will live! I was considered a miracle baby! I was always embraced with expressions, oh my dear child, you almost died, had you not drunk all that milk. This comment is followed by a tease or laughter. Sounds of my mother's gratefulness for my having lived remained a sacred memory. It indirectly impacted my having chosen religious life when I was quite young.

It takes a village to raise a child. I grew up in a village in Guam where the upbringing is centred around church activities. Social functions stemmed from religious events. When people both young and old talked, religious tones are heard in their daily utterances. God is always given credit for the effects of one's daily life in order to arrive at an understanding beyond faith and meaning. These profound recollections inspired me to take a glance at my purpose in life.

Call to the Sisterhood (1966–1983)

The high school I attended held a typical career day. Like any other high school, many different careers, professions and vocations were represented on this day so that students explored their interests and passions as an extension of the academic program. I found myself attending a presentation on Religious Life. Some Sisters observed that I was interested in Religious Life because I attended their presentations. Lo and behold, two Sisters came to my home to speak to my parents because they wanted to recruit me into considering the Sisterhood. Coming from a home life where Catholic culture and traditions with activities growing up Catholic, made it easy for me to seriously consider becoming a Sister. I always had an admiration for the Sisters who taught me, never realised, however, that I would one day become one of them. I frequented visiting the convent as I was always invited to many religious functions. I was attracted to many reflections of happiness radiated by the Sisters. Their convent home displayed a soothing ambience of holiness and stillness, and there was a blessed aroma from the chapel to the convent's hallways, dining room and into the community room where the Sisters had nightly recreation. It was a luxury of a different kind, a powerhouse for me. I heard the bells of the convent ringing in my heart calling me to be one of those young girls who wanted to serve God. I was certainly attracted to take on a journey toward holiness as I always yearned for a closer relationship with God anyways. Back then, girls who desired to become Sisters joined the Aspiranture, a convent boarding school for high school girls. Its purpose was to provide girls with a glimpse of the convent lifestyle. We put aside private telephones and private rooms in exchange for dormitories, yet when a bunch of girls got together you can be assured that there was so much fun at prayers, meals, and recreational activities. We enjoyed each other's company and how we all immediately bonded while following the rules of Mercy Life. The morning rising bell woke us to every new day with: Let us bless the Lord, and our response: Thanks be to God. Had to get all dressed in fifteen minutes, and had no time to think about time in front of mirrors and make-up. We prayed the Angeles as we walked uphill to the chapel for our daily mass, but for most of us, it really was a way to finally wake up. After the celebration of the Eucharist in the community, we had breakfast and dishes put away, all in silence so we can listen to the voice of God. It was soon time to get on the Mercy bus that would take us to our high school. A Sister began our ride with: Our Lady of the Highways, pray for us, and then we recited the rosary together. We were always glad when we finished because we were then able to engage in conversation and laughter along the way. Our whole day was spent in the classrooms. Once school was out, we drove home, we had classes on spirituality, sometimes charisms of the foundress of the Sisters of Mercy, housekeeping reminders and appropriate demeanour becoming of Sisters, followed by communal recreation and study hall where we did our homework. Bedtime was distinctive with Great Silence and lights off by 10:00. This was our daily routine in the Aspiranture. Every weekend our families came for visitation, they usually brought us a basketful of our favourite treats to share with the other aspirants. We went home on the first Sunday of every month. It was neat to revisit home with our families and reconnect with old friends. There was always a picnic gathering at the beach welcoming us home. Obviously, families, relatives, and friends were eager to hear about our life as Aspirants. For Aspirants who thought the convent life was not for them, they did not return to the Aspiranture at the end of the visitation.

After seeking help from a spiritual director and talking to Sisters, I have discerned, thought about, and prayed so much about how God moved me in my life. It was time to accept my calling which I consider a gift from God. In my freshmen year in college, I pursued joining the Congregation. That meant getting the application form and along with it, I received a supply list and clothing needs. I was told to get a physical examination and was expected to bring a dowry to my entrance day at the convent. My mother and I shopped for all my needs, it was a long list and I waited for Dad's many pay days before I could get all the items from the list. My mom was already sensing that her right arm will soon no longer be available. She cut my little sister's beautiful long hair, her hands were full looking after five children and will not have time to braid it. I was obviously going to be missed, I basically ignored this situation. It was exciting on my part getting ready for the big day for I also knew the Sisters could hardly wait to receive me into their lives. Once I entered the Novitiate, training into the candidacy gave direction to religious and professional aspirations on the Works of Mercy: nursing, teaching, serving the poor, the uneducated, and the sick I chose to become a teaching Sister as opposed to the other fields of Mercy. From the very first day, I worked with the children in Catechism classes, where I did my first teaching, it was apparent that I had found my passion for teaching. I also received compliments from the pastor who heard me teaching. How I cherished working with the students! I had two aunts who were teachers and while growing up my mom always told me how I reminded her of her two sisters. What made teaching great is I had great students. I attended classes in Elementary Education at the University of Guam and Viterbo College in La Crosse, Wisconsin. As soon as I pursued my Elementary Ed. Training, I taught children from all grade levels over the years. These students turned our classroom into a garden of learning. With zeal and compassion, I taught them the basics of Reading, Writing, Language, and Religion, a Christian approach to life, which is a call to living faith through spreading the Word. Many social activities allowed students to get to know each other whereby they found a common bond of love and fellowship. Teamwork happened during all school functions during class project presentations, at field trips, play days, lunch time in the cafeteria, and cultural performances. We held enrichment activities which helped students become more engaged in their learning and in retaining information.

Teaching is a wholly beautiful work of God for the youths of my island and its people. I loved to teach the world to sing! At the end of each teaching day, I returned to our convent home. We prayed the Divine Office communally, then spent private prayers, watched the nightly news and favourite TV programs, did sing-a-longs, corrected papers, or reviewed our lessons for the next teaching day. We put our lives on the table sharing the day's stories about the classroom and more. I enjoyed communal life and prayer with the Sisters I lived with. Throughout the years, we helped and inspired each other to be saints of our times. From our convent home to the community at large in our village neighbourhoods is the Church, the people of God whom we served. We were symbols of stewardship and dedication by reaching out and touching hearts in this labour of LOVE. There were many festivities international and local, school functions, workshops, conferences, prayer services, and church feasts. There were funerals, hospital and jail visitations, and family get-togethers. weddings, birthdays, baptisms, and anniversaries. Living on such a tiny island, you were able to make it to any of the events since none of them was too far to attend.

Oblivious to not knowing what tomorrow will bring, many years later, I found myself changing. I started to feel so confined in my ideas. I sensed the need to move on to a wider world, unlike the small community I have come to know as a Sister. I began a strong desire to extend myself beyond the convent life, restlessness filled my life. I started to question my religious calling. I once asked the congregation in an assembly why we were stripping off our habits little by little. First, it was to shorten our veils and our habits, then we added pastel colours, and before long, the habits and the veils became optional. So much emphasis on individual expression, but what about communal expressions of being united in the name of Christ who has called us into a religious community. I felt the habit was symbolic of consecration and membership in the congregation. These are externals but I believed they are important symbols that separated us from the laity. It is important to have a visible sign to remind people that God lives in our world. Yet, I saw that the goals of the congregation were more on blending in with the laity. It seems to me that the Sisters do not want to dare to be different as witnesses of Christ's followers. If I did not dress like a Sister, so why be a Sister? As I observed uncertainties in communal living, I was having my own questions about being in the convent in the first place. In Catholic schools, we told our students that uniform gives discipline to every student. Our students behaved differently when they were not in uniform. Habits worn by Sisters gave way to responsible leadership as the habit we wore was a reminder of who we represented every day. Aside from my dissatisfaction with these changes, I also encountered other inclinations. We always had entertainment by our students for different school functions, one performance made an impact on me and took me into a world I never knew. Over the years, the music teacher always provided musical accompaniment for my students' presentations. In one of these special performances, he came to tell me that all those students on stage are beautiful like you and he squeezed my hand and told me so. This human touch forever changed me as I felt electricity run through me after all I was attracted to him. I felt different altogether, a feeling I never ever had before that unique day. I was a virgin touched for the very first time and this awesome feeling taught me what love looked like. The council members of my community decided to reassign me. This was to allow myself to get away from the situation I encountered and to forget the situation ever happened. A transfer was supposedly good for me! My Mother Superior told me it was all temptation; however, I could not heed to her advice. I did not pray to St. Joseph who was the guardian of those who embraced holy virginity. Back then I did not have any devotion to Saint Joseph, nor did I know that he was the patron for sensual urges or desires for sexual pleasures. So, as the song goes from the Sound of Music: "How Do You Solve a Problem Like Maria?" No matter how I prayed, I already knew I must follow the beat of my heart because I was not at peace with myself. I have moved away from the situation, but I still carried with me the same heart and soul, I was still in turmoil, I was not changed. The separation did not seem to be the answer to my restlessness. This unsettling feeling continued; this new power directed me out there somewhere. I yearned for marriage, to find a man who would make me whole. I dreamed to share life and to serve God through the companionship of one man whom I envisioned will make me a stronger woman. I pursued wholesome fulfilment and curiosity as I was discovering myself; l embraced my experience with this new awareness. I was sexually awakened and knew I must respond to what my body is saying to me. I was no longer asking myself whether it is the right thing to do, but I saw the need to follow my heart. I was afraid of the unknown as it unwrapped itself to me, but my fears lessened as I prayed and arrived at believing that God will hold me in the palm of His hand. I found strength in temptation and I trusted that these uncertainties would unfold. Wisdom allowed me to accept all the unknown.

The sisters who lived with me in the community gave me so much support in the new choice I was making. They were opened with my desire to leave and promised to pray for me. One of them even told me that I was so brave after all it took a lot of courage to declare that I wanted out of the convent. When I was a young Sister, I recalled my children's fathers at parent-teacher conferences who commented, what are you doing in the convent, you could make a man happy, you do not belong in a convent. My father always told me, I need to get out of there, that is 'only' a temporary life. He did not see me happy! He saw so many Sisters come and go! I think he wished that I leave the convent before I got too old to start a family. I looked back and saw how their comments were so unfair, but they did make sense to me so many years later. I have grown into womanhood! The little girl in me wanted to be a Sister, but now I put those notions behind me. I made the decision to become a Sister when I was too young to plan my life forever.

I would recommend training in the Religious Life to any woman, I have no regrets, it was the best place to spend my young life and I remain grateful for the years I gave to Religious Life. I received religious, domestic, and professional training all in one, in other words becoming a whole person. Many beautiful years as a Sister entrusted me to be the woman I am today, it shaped me into who I am. Old habits die hard! I still have God in my heart. I will always be a woman of God, serving Him in all circumstances of my life. In my life as a Sister of Mercy, however, MANY ARE CALLED, and a FEW ARE CHOSEN. I felt that I did not have an authentic religious vocation. I responded to an inner voice from within me desiring to walk with God along a different path. After much integrity and discernment, I asked for exclaustration. While waiting to have the official papers processed, I went shopping for new wardrobes with my mother superior, how beautiful was that! It was certainly a shopping trip I would never forget. She too was so excited seeing me try on all these dresses at the shopping mall. There I was an adult woman but felt like a little girl in a brand-new dress! The last days in the convent were filled with mixed emotions as the Sisters embraced me with blessings for the future ahead of me. I was advised to go into graduate school so I can support myself financially believing that a graduate degree will allow me to have a comfortable life. Nobody expected that I would find a husband, but I knew exactly what I wanted. My mother superior told me that one day she hoped to see me blossom into a happy woman. I thought of The Sound of Music, I am truly Maria in real life. It is no longer "How Do You Solve a Problem Like Maria," it was me answering the call: Here I am Lord I do not know where I am going but I am on my way to a wide and open universe! It was time to get on eagle's wings and I sensed a new coming dawn. I responded to the song from The Sound of Music which awakened me to a new reality. That beautiful wedding gown was symbolic of how I put aside my 'habit' to declare a new function in my world. I entertained the thought of walking down the church aisle as someone's bride one day. The song Here Comes the Bride was becoming real too! The narrative of The Sound of Music defined me because, like Maria, I wanted something beyond the horizons of convent life. Like Maria, I also felt the religious life was my calling, but later felt that life does not suit me anymore, I was no longer happy. We both left the convent yet holding on to a service ministry which we continued into our new walk of life. She, a governess and a singer, teaching children to sing, and I, a teacher teaching students in a public-school setting. I pursued my teaching career with a mainstream group of learners rather than a selective group who went to Catholic Schools. This grand scheme into public life felt wonderful, it looked so big with so much exploration. I felt the freedom to be who I wanted to be, the freedom to make choices within the confines of my own heart and soul. Newness was wholeheartedly meant to be!

On my way back to Guam, my first stop over was in California where I spent time with an incredibly special cousin. One of the first things I did was got my ears pierced and bought me my first pair of earrings. Jewellery was my first declaration to set me apart from being a Sister. The only jewellery I wore as a Sister was a plain silver ring and a cross necklace. How I loved my earrings! My cousin was so excited about styling my hair to make me look like Sandra Dee and then she laughed. I remembered being so nervous when I attended a party at the Queen Mary. As soon as I got to Guam, my nieces and nephews were taught to address me as Auntie Mare, not Sister Mare and of course, I felt funny with my new title, it did not feel like me. My greatest support came from my family! I lived with my brother and his family till I gained financial independence six months later. I welcomed my new endeavours! I moved into my own apartment and was so thrilled to have my own place and my new friends come to visit me. They were no longer friends or benefactors of the convent community, but friends I have chosen. My friends beyond the convent were a few single women, some married and many were newly divorced. They were ready to do the matchmaking! Obviously, they knew where I was coming from!! Lots of double dating took place and of course, I fathom every adventure. My friends all were very inclined to share some pointers about how not to let a man get by with his bad habits. They said if he leaves his shoes in the middle of the living room, immediately tell him to put them in their appropriate place, do not wait till six months later. They told me some men do not put the toothpaste caps or the toilet seats back in place, so they say, you must train your man from the start. These touches of humour amused me, yet they were little rules to go by! I was also told to find a man who is close to his mother, such a man will know how to treat women right. By the way, I did have the Sisters over to see my home once I was all settled in after all they will always be my first friends, my first family. They described my new home as a perfect dollhouse, everything in place, decorated simply, and it looked immaculately clean. What do you expect, no children, no grandchildren, no dogs, nor cats? I called my first apartment a playhouse! No more vows of poverty, chastity and obedience to live by! Let me add, these vows, however, prepared me for the facts of life, to take care of myself and to become whole. Jesus still remained tucked in my heart; I so needed His direction. My entire life had now become personal, I own my own car, I did not have to ask for permission to get the key nor do I have to share it with anyone. I could shop for any style and colours of wardrobe, short or long dresses, low necklines or spaghetti straps, whatever I desired. Most of all I earned my money and now I have the freedom to take care of myself instead of depending on community life to cater to my needs. I was so elated as I anticipated my first pay check! Before I ever received my first pay check, I had made a list of things I wanted. My family teased me that I needed my second and maybe a third and fourth pay check for I had such a long list. The first thing I bought was my car. I told my big brother that I wanted a cheap car with air conditioning, four doors, and an automatic shift. He told me that does not come cheap, he was amused since he was dealing with someone with no experience in selecting cars and having money. He also taught me how to balance my chequebook and many more new responsibilities expected of an independent woman. Any woman who had spent many years in a convent needs to learn one's re-entry into secular life. I was learning so much in my newness of life and I had to let my life unfold overnight. The transition was both exciting and mind-blowing.

The Sisters genuinely wanted me to teach with them, but I was determined to provide myself with a new perspective in life and be as far away from my convent friends as possible. Most Sisters who left the convent hung out with the Sisters because it was safe. I still love them of course but I just wanted to seek new acquaintances, especially with men, make more money than what a private school had to offer, as well as establish my new role in life with all its challenges. I was open to confronting all that is before me and I was professionally prepared to resume responsibilities on my own. Now is the time to navigate my life and have the internal fortitude to believe in myself. I stepped into a public elementary school for the first time and the principal gladly welcomed a product of a Catholic School into her staff. I found new friendships in the public-school community. My co-workers were glad that I have joined them because they envisioned these children needed a true Christian woman like me. These students were from low economic neighbourhoods who deserved so much support. I found myself working with the poorest of the poor and the most disadvantaged children of the community. I arrived at my calling to serve students in need. I believe that Jesus called me once again, "a call within a call", but this time to embrace a calling into public life! The discipline and structure I brought into our classroom made a positive influence on these learners. I am not a new person; I am the same teacher delivering knowledge to young learners. Students loved my teaching style and I developed a rapport with them. I empowered students to take responsibility for their learning and preparing them for a future ahead of them. I modelled leadership through caring and loving them as individuals, teaching them values of honesty, and generosity, and most importantly, I taught them to welcome diversity into our classroom. These charisms would assist them in becoming whole persons in this challenging world we all live in. When you enjoy what you do, it becomes a reflection on the students you teach. My sister always told me, that every new school year you tell me that you love your class. There was never a group you did not enjoy. Well, I love teaching and showed it too!

I met my best friend outside the convent at the Reading Teachers Association meeting. Her first question to me was why you are not married, she said that she asked everyone who was single the same question after all she was single herself. We immediately clicked and we became dear friends. We always visited each other's homes over wine after a long teaching day. We shared many stories together! Being a Reading teacher, she surely was a storyteller, and our nightly conversations made the evenings go by quickly. When the cockroaches came out of the kitchen cabinet, we then knew it was time to end the evening's visit and count on the next day's visit. One evening she suggested that we go off-island to pursue graduate work. For her, it was her doctorate degree, and for me, it was my master's degree. I held back thinking I just was not smart enough to go to graduate school. We had good long discussions about this, in the end, she says, you know Mare, we can both find a husband in the USA. I flew with that thought, I was so delighted and ready for that! The decision to go abroad ended up being a very smart move, a foreseeable future indeed. We applied at three different universities, first, it was to the University of Virginia since that was the first university in America, we wanted a place that had a history in the making. Then, I picked the University of New Mexico and the University of Arizona since I was interested in Second Language

Teaching. I got accepted at the University of Arizona, and acceptance to the University of New Mexico came later after I was already attending the University of Arizona. The University of Virginia did not accept us because it already met the quota with the number of international students attending. My sister asked me how could I just pick up and leave. I told her that I spoke English, and loved meeting people and making new friends. I also knew I will go to a Catholic Church to meet people like me. Everything happened as planned, grateful for life! I had a friend who told me, Mare, nobody can stop you with what you want to do, just do it. Those promptings from a good teacher friend had always been my motto in my life's choices.

College Life, Marriage, and Life in Indiana (1986–1988)

Setting foot into a desert on the West Coast, where Suahiro cactus have stood seven hundred years old or more, I arrived here with the goal of studying English as a Second Language. I embarked on my journey of studying ESL at the University of Arizona in Tucson. While attending the University I met people from every part of the world all representing a native lingua both familiar and unfamiliar. I found myself immersed with teachers from around the world with one common goal: to teach English to speakers of other languages. Our target language was English, this was our mode of communication in our educational settings and in our social lives. Many varied and shared experiences from cultures around the world were truly an awakening to my first global experience. The best time of my life happened here! Not only did we share knowledge and ideas about ESL teaching and methodology, but we also exchanged each other's customs and traditions from our respective countries which were all symbolic of growing friendships. Being at the university gave me an opportunity to make lifelong connections with fellow classmates from different backgrounds and cultures. I was forever learning!

I ventured my way around the university campus and explored the city by bus. I rode my bike to all my classes on this huge campus. I found the Newman Centre as my place of worship and made new friends at its different functions. In the next semester, my good friend from Guam joined me at the University. I brought her to the new apartment I had reserved for her. She was so excited to see how beautiful it was with so much space all to herself, she also liked the area. How wonderful it was to have someone from Guam studying with me. Having her just made living in Tucson a much nicer place to be. We both enjoyed each other's company sometimes over a Guam meal, going shopping by bus, or visiting restaurants around the university area. My friends became her friends too and there were many social gatherings in place to give ourselves a break from research papers, and exams. and many other class assignments. We observed the different strokes of American women in our midst. We both cherished transitioning into independent living through home management, budgeting, and setting routines so there is a balance between student life and personal life.

It did not take long into my second semester, while seated across in the library, my ears listened to the silences and glances profoundly penetrated each other. These silences and glances kept taking me back to the same spot in the library where I would find a special person. On the early morning of our first meeting day, my long hair appeared wet from having come out of the shower. He said, to himself, this is the woman I wanted, she looked much older than the girls I ever dated. She cannot be young since young students do not go to the library till real late into the night. He said young girls walked out on him, he figured an older woman knew what she wanted. To this day we still grapple with which one of us smiled first when we first saw each other in the library that morning. To this day, neither of us has given in! One day we finally decided to go out together. He had just finished a test and needed to get off campus for a while. I found a friend, not realising he would become my best friend, my significant other for life. This first date was at a Chinese Restaurant situated right across the University of Arizona campus. It was a delightful dinner of course. We exchanged messages from our fortune cookies. His message said: the man you are with has volume. Mine read: you will find great fortune in unexpected places. We welcomed peers to join us in our friendship journey. We all participated in many entertaining activities at the Newman Centre, attended football games, watched movies on campus, or explored restaurants in town whenever we were not in study groups preparing for exams or project presentations. Our life's focus was on our field of study, so much time devoted to studying, cramming, discovering, learning, and relearning theories and doing research. One must grasp all knowledge and select ideas which will enhance our field work for the future. My significant other was in engineering school, but we chose the linguistic library for our meeting place to do our studies. He wanted to tell me in my native language, "Chamorro", how he viewed me. He searched for the Chamorro dictionary in the Linguistic Library. He looked up what he wanted to communicate to me, the first words he wanted to say to me in my native language. I thought, how impressive and loving was such a gesture. Language is as intimate as a mother's heart is to her child. That was a "wow" moment to have received this note written to me in my native language which said: Carinosa hao yan dudos hao, meaning you are a very charming and flirtatious woman. It touched the deepest level of my beating heart, I was falling in love indeed, and our friendship continued to nurture. On one of our many walks together, I told him of a classmate who impressed me so much because she was so kind, so generous, and so loving, just like a Sister. He immediately asked, "How do you know how Sisters were supposed to act?" And I told him that I had been a Sister. That was the moment of revelation! He said he has been a little confused because I am a woman, but such a little girl, I am intelligent but quite naïve, I have so much strength, but very fragile, and I am so charming but quite reserved. He described me as impulsively romantic and now that answered all his questions! He was not at all afraid, he was so proud to know where I was coming from. I told him I have a picture of me as a Sister in my living room, I never hid this from you. He said yes, I saw the picture, but I thought you were wearing a costume for a school play. This comment apparently revealed to me that he is a non-Catholic. Incidentally at that moment, he told me I must treat you well because you are God's favoured one. As he got to know me more, he started buying me new clothes fitting the sign of the times as he thought my clothes were old-fashioned. Hey, I am nearly twenty years behind the times, getting back to where I left off. It was like I have been asleep for twenty years and just woke up to live in a world totally different. Don was very patient with me as I had so much catching up to do in my new world. I was a woman in the process! I felt the Lord empowering me to move on to a new direction in life. As the days became weeks, weeks became months, and months became years, so much exchange was happening in our relationship. One day it was time to be introduced to his grandparents living in Arizona and later, to his family in Indiana. I, from "Guam, Where America's Day Begins", and he from Indiana, the "Crossroads of America". So far away from these places and yet so close, a world tied together in one miraculous motion. We shared many meals together, so his folks got to know me. It was incredibly challenging as I felt I was being scrutinised, but normal of course, after all their son and I were having a serious relationship. I was the first person they had met outside the rural small-town America they live in. Don's little niece and nephews readily accepted me for the person that I was right away. They had no reservations about talking to me, such is the innocence and simplicity of children. On one of my walks with Don's mother in Tucson one evening after dinner, she picked up a wedding favour she had found on the ground, she smiled and gave it to me with a big, friendly smile. This wedding favour she had found was representative of her acceptance of me. I believed she anticipated the two of us getting married.

Don moved back to Indiana while I still had a year of graduate school. We gave birth to a long-distance relationship. Two hearts becoming one as friendship is deepened with time! Many letters and many phone calls made the heart grow fonder in our long-distance relationship. Engagement became our next proclamation to a love growing together as one. There was nothing romantic about how I received my ring. No red roses, wine and chocolates over a romantic candlelight dinner. He said what you see is what you get, obviously, he was a plain and simple guy. He put my ring in a beautifully decorated twelve-inch sealed can and handed it to me at the shopping mall where we selected it. He laughingly handed me a can opener, so I opened the can, and he made his proposal and put the ring on my finger. How cleverly unique was that! At a mass at the Newman Centre, my best friend from Guam saw my sparkling diamond ring. She asked me during the mass, "Oh my God are you engaged?"

Long did she ever know, I would choose her to be my maid of honour. Don chose his brother as his best man. Months ahead meant wedding plans! Wedding bells rang and families from Indiana, Germany, Guam, and college best friends joined us for our nuptial ceremony. A wedding celebration under one hundred fourteen degrees in the heat of July in the desert was almost unbearable for our guests. The things family and good friends did for us! It was dry heat alright, still, nobody welcomed the sun of Tucson that day. The celebration started with a beautiful high mass at the Newman Centre at the University of Arizona. The reception was held at the elegant casita-like style property of Arizona Inn Resort. After the reception, my father asked me, "When are you coming home?" Dad forgot that I am now married and would be moving to my new home in Indiana. You should have seen the look on his face. I wanted to remind him that he had just walked me down the aisle, Dad, you gave me away, but I chose not to remind him. After the wedding party, our first night as a married man and woman was under heavy storms. Flash of lightning and booming thunder bolted from the sky above Ventana Canyon. My new husband carried me up the stairwells and flipped me down into the bed. I recalled this gigantic bedroom with a bathroom which included a bathtub that looked deeper than the Pacific Ocean I once knew. I felt safe and beautiful! The first week of our honeymoon was spent there before we continued the next ten days driving in our Ryder truck carrying all our belongings all the way to the Hoosier State. It was one of a kind of a honeymoon with the Ryder truck taking us across the country from Tucson, Arizona to Valparaiso, Indiana. Our first stop was at the scenic

Grand Canyon which was a sight to behold with all the beautiful colours of rock layers. Here we were in one of the world's natural wonders. We continued into Utah the following day, where we found ourselves in six per cent grade roadways. Don decided that it was my turn to drive. Naively I accepted the responsibility! I only knew the hills of my island home, Guam. Maybe I do remember the hills of Austria from watching the movie The Sound of Music, little did I realise what I was getting into. The saddest, lowest part of our honeymoon placed us at the bottom of the six per cent grade with a flat tire. This was our tale of woe as we found ourselves in the middle of nowhere in the desert. The buzzers watched us as we sat on the bumper of the truck wondering what we were going to do next. How are we to get any help? Lo and behold, a car came by and rescued us. The people at first were apprehensive about helping us, but I guessed we looked like fine people after all. This stranger picked Don up and took him to the nearest gas station, I stayed behind and waited. Don returned to me in a motorcycle, his first ride on one. How blessed we were to have gotten help! The next city herein our honeymoon journey was Denver, Colorado. As we drove into Denver, Colorado, the rays of the rainbow in dazzling colours formed an arch from the valley down low where we were driving, and up to the mountaintops of Denver. Surely this was a promise of a beautiful marriage ahead of us! The rainbow was so cool, and it lasted a long time! We left Colorado and continued to Nebraska to the Black Hills of the Dakotas. I wanted to see the place where the Black Hills jewellery was made. Women in his family, his two sisters and mother wore Black Hills jewellery, a kind of jewellery unknown to me till I first met him. Yellow gold was the gold worn by Pacific Island women like me. I immediately found a new liking for

Black Hills Gold. My wedding band was Black Hills gold and so was my necklace for that special day. We left the Dakotas and arrived in Sioux Falls, Iowa, with a direct east drive to Dubuque. This was the place where I ate my waffle topped with peaches and whipped cream during my first winter wonderland experience. I was on a trip with friends from Viterbo College in Wisconsin many years before I met him. Our honeymoon was a trip celebrating memories of places we have been to. This trip was getting us closer to our first home together as husband and wife. When we left Iowa, Don wanted to show me Rockford, Illinois where he worked five years before he met me. He had wanted to stop at a hotel there, but on this trip, I learned one thing about my new husband, he does not plan anything, everything is impromptu. Lo and behold, there were no hotels available anywhere in Rockford or its nearby cities. This cut our honeymoon short, so it was time to head to Valparaiso, Indiana. It was all flatlands from Illinois to Indiana. Yes, indeed, the flatlands gave way to a good description of my new home to be. Arriving in Valparaiso, our Ryder truck was parked in the driveway of our first home. A rural setting for an island girl was just the right place for me. Neighbours were all on the lookout to peek at the bride Don brought back home to Valparaiso, Indiana. Neighbours were curious, they all said he never lived in that house because he travelled all the time for his job. Now a wife will keep the house lived in. A wedding is a day, followed by a week or so of honeymooning, now marriage is a lifetime. The first thing we did was unload our possessions from Tucson into our Valparaiso home. Don's mother was afraid that we brought the bugs from Arizona into Indiana. Therefore, we carefully unpacked our boxes making sure no critters came for the ride into Hoosier land. A home is a place where when you get

51

there, you walk right in. Don opened the door and I followed behind. I bumped into a decoration at the front door, and I broke it. I guessed I was nervous, excited, and a little clumsy to have pushed the door hard enough to break his knickknack. He was so upset!! For a second, I felt like going out the door back to my island home in Guam. Our life's aspirations as two hearts becoming one started right at this front door, ugh, seeing how my new husband overreacted. Whoa! I guessed he was so tired from the long journey. Real-life set in, this man had a temper. We both put things away and relaxed in our home. The following week, Don goes back to work while I did a job search. The first person I networked with was a priest whom I introduced myself to at my first Sunday mass at a Catholic church in Valparaiso. I told him that I am an experienced teacher from Guam looking for a job. He told me to come into his office Monday and fill out the application form. No sweat, I found myself at the right time and right place! He happened to be the Superintendent of Schools. My husband declared that I was one lucky lady and for the last thirty-two years, he still thinks I am a lucky lady. I declared it was the grace of God taking hold of me because I believe that I am a woman of God. I smiled at my world and the world smiled back at me. Teaching days followed at St. Mary of the Lake for the first year and the following year the superintendent asked me if I still wanted to teach at St Paul school where I wanted to work at first. There were no positions available at the time I applied. I met beautiful families who had good children who were all curious to know a teacher from outside the country. I received a grand welcome from the children, staff, and parents of the St. Paul school community. It was so exciting, stepping into a mid-western classroom with mid-western hospitality. Having found myself in a classroom is my kind of world, I love to teach the world to sing. So much interaction happened among parents, students, and the staff as I hoped to belong in this rural small-town school community. A teacher friend in this Valparaiso neighbourhood met me at a corner every morning on our walk to school. It was so amazingly homey having a teacher friend in the neighbourhood. We clicked right away; she was a good person to me. I told her lots of stories about Guam; she was sharing her life in this small town. She was so amused that I wore my long winter coat in early October. Oh well, it is the island girl in me, this is what the tropics have done for me, I was so cold. Some things in life you just take one day at a time. Guam has the American school system, so the curriculum is not totally different, the major difference is in the seasonal activities of the Mid-west.

That same year, I was so blessed to have had a second job in Adult Ed. about thirty miles from our home, in Portage, Indiana. Once again, a job was almost handed over to me since the program needed someone with Second Language Learning expertise. I continued to make new friends in the areas where I lived and worked. The population I worked with were migrants who worked on the farm and that was my first grasp into ESL teaching. It was so rewarding teaching them! They were trying to make a living in the USA. It was a wholly wonderful ministry to assist people who are transitioning to an understanding of the American culture and its language. ESL techniques became handy as I worked to reach them and to make them comfortable in learning the basic skills of reading, writing, and speaking. I taught them survival skills for living in the USA: what to say at the supermarket and to identify names of items when shopping, what to say at the banks, at the clinic, and many other places in the community. I taught them appropriate language and behaviour for many other community services and businesses. These students taught me more about Second Language Teaching than what any book has presented in its pedagogical approaches. Experience lends to further expertise! ESL classroom with adults has social emphasis, we sat around the table to study the language for that is how I got them to practice conversation. We always had coffee and doughnuts or coffee and cookies at breaktimes. Everything on the table was labelled so vocabulary use is enhanced. The most exciting part about working with migrants is their motivation to learn. They were beautiful humble people! By the way, I had my first winter experience at this time, my students learned survival language, and I learned how to survive in the snow. Students with their teachers adjusting to a different world!

In the course of time, I adjusted to the culture and traditions of the family I am married in. When you marry a man, you also marry his family. Every Sunday we had breakfast with his parents, and then drove all over town to look at houses. This was their way of looking at the changes in different parts of town, while also enjoying and envying how the wealthy build their dream homes. They were quite fond of looking at the characters of each of the houses. This was a whole new experience for me. By the time we bought our first home, I knew what to look for in a house.

We both engaged in learning to live together. I worked hard at being a house manager! I would fill up the freezer with meat and found out that the meat at our table must come fresh from the butcher shop down the street from our home. No frozen meats in this household, unlike when I lived on Guam meat was imported frozen daily from Australia, New

Zealand, or the U.S. Mainland. Meals on the table must also be piping hot! I had forgotten I was in a cold country, he wanted piping hot food on the table. These are a few housekeeping rules that I learned from my new husband. He too learned to have rice daily and found soy sauce as a staple in our kitchen cabinets. Let me add, we added coconut flavours to our meals. One time, two times, three times I sent him to the supermarket to get a coconut. Each time he came home, the coconut he bought was rotten. What does a man from the Mid-west know about coconuts! I decided to get the coconut myself. I took a machete with me to the produce section of the supermarket. I asked the man from this produce department to give me a coconut. He took a hammer to cut it open. I said, no let me show you how to split open a coconut the way we do on the islands. I turned the machete opposite the blade side, the heavier side of the machete to cut it open. He was not only amused that I brought a machete to open the coconut, but that I turned the machete upside down to cut it open. I told my story of the day to Don. He was so upset with me, I guess that was our first fight in our marriage. That temper happened again! He told me how lucky I was that the police were not called to handcuff me and to take me to the police station where he had to bail me out from jail, the woman with a machete. He declared; woman grow up you are not in the convent anymore; this world is not a safe place. You cannot walk in this town with a machete in your hand. Other life's learnings in the rural town where I first lived involved learning to drive in the snow. Don took me to a big open parking space at a high school near our neighbourhood. He made me practice being behind the wheel in the snow, I felt so intimidated. I also received advice about driving on bridges and all the caution I must take. One day he got me behind the wheel and said let us go for a drive, this was my first time on the expressway. I drove far, then I noticed aeroplanes and guess how far he took me on this drive, all the way to O'Hare Airport, two hours away from our home. What a guy! Most teachers share their stories with their students. The next day, I told my students that my husband was teaching me how to drive in the snow and on the expressway, and they told me about making angels in the snow. This opened the door to further comparative discussions on what it was like living in Guam and living in Valparaiso. My students taught me a lot through exchanging ideas. Their eyes opened in amazement when I told them the highest speed limit in Guam is forty-five miles per hour and that the whole island of Guam can sit on top of Porter County, and still have lots of room. They could not imagine how tiny it was and they opened their mouths in awe.

In only the second year of our marriage, I received the news I did not want to hear; my husband was going to be transferred to Puerto Rico, so we had a long-distance relationship once again. I continued my job with teaching but travelled to Puerto Rico on every school holiday. This was a wholly wonderful arrangement since it was quite tough being separated as we were newlyweds. Most of all, lesson plans and school functions kept me busy. I visited with his parents and my best friend kept me company as well. She shared her family of three lovely children and made me quite at home visiting and spending time with them. They lived on a farm, so I certainly learned about all the responsibilities of farm life in Indiana. It was interesting to eat meals from farm to table. I often had them over at my house to treat them to a Guam meal. The following year, Don called me on a Good Friday to tell me that he will resign from his job in Puerto Rico so that he could come home to go to church with me.

Don knew my favourite place and so chose this as his reason for coming home. We missed each other terribly! It was the best Easter gift. To this day, we still go to church together every Sunday. In the over thirty years of marriage, he travelled away from home for his job for about half the time in our marriage. Every time we were together, it was a gift, every homecoming was a honeymoon all over again. Let me add, however, there were still adaptations to living together again. I was becoming independent of him and settled in my ways. We had to make many adjustments, but we managed life as it was. He said when he came home, all the chores he used to do were done and obviously felt his routine was taken away. He had forgotten he has a wife to keep the house, yeah me, the house manager. With so much energy, I did both indoor and outdoor chores. I figured if I did all the chores, then we can spend quality time together and do fun things once he got home.

Two years later, we moved to Indianapolis because of my husband's change of jobs again. The best part about it is that it is a little warmer than living in the snow belts of Valparaiso. Secondly, finding myself in a metropolitan city provided me with the opportunity to do ESL teaching. While my husband reported to his new job, I sent in applications to many school districts. My first job in Indianapolis was an Outreach Program in Washington Township. I taught ESL in the morning to seventy senior citizens from Russia who came to Indianapolis as refugees. The Jewish Community Centre sponsored their arrival in Indianapolis. Most of them were retired engineers from Russia. I was introduced to Russian culture, while I also observed my students' learning styles. My teacher assistant was from Russia too and he was the first friend I ever had from this country. It was so much fun working with him since he played the guitar and we learned so much English through singing. There I was again making friends with a musician. Music was in the air in our classroom and what a fun way to learn a new language. He shared a lot of his learning experiences in having come to the United States. When he first came, he did not change clothes daily. One thing that stood out is how there is so much water in the United States and unlike in his country, people took showers and changed their clothes every day here. Some things in life we take for granted!! I also taught family literacy in the evening. It was amazing teaching parents and their children together; the children had the advantage of learning English since they spent six hours a day in regular school. They were picking up the language much faster than their parents which somehow embarrassed their parents. I had to bring comfort to the parents and advised the students to be humble mentors to their parents. Two years later, there was an opening for a full-time ESL teaching position. I went into the Adult Basic Education in IPS. The population of the students I worked with in my classes represented every part of the world. I taught in this program for nearly twenty years. We had two full-time day class sessions, of which I worked in one. The rest were all held in the evenings for the working population. Both day and evening classes flourished, and I also taught at night. How I loved this job! Being a second language learner myself, entrusted me with this awesome responsibility.

Why I Chose this Profession

How in the world did I end up being an English Teacher for Speakers of Other Languages? Well, everything that we do in life is dictated by who we are as individuals. A classroom situation can make an impact on a child's life! In my case, these situations regarded a classmate of mine who liked stealing lunches. How enticing my lunch boxes which my mom prepared for me every day, must have looked to this classmate! Each lunch period I opened my lunch box, but my sandwich was not there because someone helped himself to it. My mother told me how to report this incident to my teacher. She said, tell your teacher: teacher somebody took my lunch. For someone like me who hardly spoke English, I memorised what to report to my teacher. In school the following day, I told her: teacher, you stole my lunch. It was so traumatic to have insulted my teacher. My teacher sent a note home to my mother which said please speak English to your daughter. My mom responded back, you teach my daughter English in school, and I will teach her our home language. This was my memory of what led me to become an English Teacher to Speakers of Other languages. There was no ESL field at the time I was a child in school. I wanted to step beyond an academic system that did not adequately help me to learn to speak English. I did not want children to go through the same experience. I wanted to do it differently. I had this heart-driven intent to assist students in their learning of English so that they could communicate well in their classrooms. I embraced a passion for teaching English to Speakers of Other Languages.

Another experience which inspired me in this career was the influx of foreign visitors to Guam at the time I was a public school elementary teacher there. Guam is the closest to the heart of the U.S. for immigrants from Japan, Korea,

Taiwan, and China. People from the Orient with high economic status were establishing businesses in Guam. This has bought an increasing number of non-English speakers to our island's schools. The schools of Guam became an ethnic rainbow. These non-English speaking students whom I had in my classroom were challenged. I ended up tutoring them after school hours. I told them that we had something in common, that I was a second language learner myself and faced the challenges of learning English. Establishing rapport with students was so, so important. I saw an opportunity to instruct my students in their new language, after all, I understand the process. At the time I was an elementary teacher, there were no trained teachers in second language learning in Guam.

When the opportunity came for me to choose a second career, I looked back on these two experiences. I moved on to a new vision in my teaching career. I visualised the need for teaching in a new field of learning. Immigrants entering our school system needed support in their second language learning. I took a path less travelled by into new methodology and innovative teaching for speakers of other languages. I wanted to be the educator who brought the mission of imparting English to students new to the English language.

Working with the Student Population
(1988–2017)

At this time, I want to identify the population of the students I worked with in my classes. Some were people coming to the U.S. as refugees. These were people from Russia, Afghanistan, Ethiopia, Haiti, and Burma. People from Saudi Arabia, Egypt, Iraq, Iran, and Africa arrived to seek educational opportunities in our American Universities. People from China, Thailand, and Africa arrived with working visas to work in American companies. The young people from Italy, Spain, and Germany arrived as au pairs. Au pairs created a global family. They provided quality, intercultural childcare for U.S. families. An au pair lives in a family home and becomes a full-fledged family member, sharing a unique cultural exchange. Our closest neighbour, Mexico, as well as people from Central America and South America, came to the U.S. in search of better lives. No matter what their reasons, they all needed English. I chose to work with students who were beginners because it was at this level that I could instil good learning habits right from the start in their attempt to learn English. I immediately told students that they must be good listeners. I brought in lots of non-verbal methods, and used gestures, real objects, videos, pictures, and flashcards for I considered these as the best methods for explaining and modelling. I did pair-work, group activities, getting to know you exercises, word searches, and language games. For newly arrived students these techniques are brand new and exciting! I always modelled everything before expecting students to take their turn in language learning. I reduced my Teacher Talk because students at this level need the simplest and most efficient explanations to understand what is being said.

When one learns a language, one needs to know the culture and traditions for which the language is spoken. I taught all the different American holidays throughout the year. I taught the game of bingo using the vocabulary words for special holidays. After having studied each, we had a celebration. Students brought their favourite foods, labelled their dishes and exchanged recipes. It was at this time that they were introduced to measurement vocabulary and the use of verbs for directions. All this made learning entertaining! They loved social functions. So much bonding took place beyond the classroom. I also had International Fairs and we invited families, friends, and neighbourhoods. Students proudly presented the flags of their countries, brought in souvenirs, and once again displayed their favourite meals. So much team building took place and whether they were aware of it or not, so much language was taking place too. This was a gala event, everyone exhibited what is typically representative of the cultures they came from. How fun it was to learn from each other's cultures!

The most eventful time of my teaching career was teaching English on TV. Its purpose was to give the working non-English speakers with conflicting work schedules who cannot attend any of our classes, the opportunity to learn English right in their own living rooms. The program is called "Crossroads Café: Indianapolis" and it was played four times daily during the hours in which these workers came home from their workplaces. I formed a round-table group of six students who had different native languages to facilitate my presentation. We rehearsed the entire lesson before being televised. My students modelled to the home viewers/learners on how the instruction was going to be carried on. The home viewers/learners followed along with my students using the Crossroads Café textbook along with supplementary materials. My presentation consisted of pre-video lessons, watching the video, and post-video lessons. The pre-video lessons included the vocabulary that students will hear during the video, the characters they will meet, and the theme for the episode they are about to watch. The theme usually contains English idioms or phrases and expressions that were difficult to understand. Students discussed what the theme meant to them. Once this part of the lesson is done, the students watched the video. After the video, there were discussion questions about the episode. The students also studied the language structure that was used in the episode.

Crossroads Café's curriculum consists of 26-episodes featuring six engaging characters and a neighbourhood restaurant. The stories portray the human drama of the challenges, struggles, and victories of everyday life in the USA. The series features diverse ethnicities, real-world scenarios familiar to many as well as universal, social, and cultural issues for family members of all ages. Each episode is accompanied by an animated video segment that demonstrates a specific language function, for example, making a complaint, talking about wants, giving compliments, talking about likes and dislikes, etc., etc. The episode is also enriched with Culture Clips, a documentary-style segment that took a close look at the social and cultural issues dramatised in the story. An American friend once told me he saw my TV presentation. I know this program is for newcomers to our country. However, watching it made me aware of everything I need to know and learn when I visit countries outside the U.S. There was an emphasis on vocabulary and language needed in a culture, all the specifics that one needs to know about a country you visit. While it was an enjoyable drama, everybody benefited from watching this TV presentation. I was grateful for the city government, my school district and the TV station which worked cooperatively to make this opportunity possible for all who could not attend English class. All viewers were enriched by an adequate grasp of American culture and traditions, the use of idioms, phrases, and expressions for casual conversations. Crossroads Café was designed with graduated levels of challenge. Learners can "grow" with Crossroads Café, using the video series over and over, revisiting episodes and the lessons at increasing levels of language proficiency.

Rewards of Teaching
Students in Their New Language

It was such an opportunity to have met students from around the globe. I know that the English language is continually growing, and close to becoming a universal language which makes it a global language. I was so proud to be a part of this transition into their new language. It was quite rewarding to see my students speak, read, and understand English. One of the most enjoyable rewards in all of the teaching was seeing the learning process happening live, dynamically in front of me. Lessons extended beyond the classroom! Students taught their parents, their friends, their siblings, and even their grandparents. It was awe-inspiring to know the gifts I had shared were passed on over and over. I had students tell me, I can help my children with their homework now. I, as their teacher, was indirectly helping another family member. My students came back to my class to tell me stories about their lives beyond the classroom. They told me my manager said I am speaking English now, or I am understanding others speak to me at my workplace. I attended a parent-teacher conference for my children without a bi-lingual translator. I watched my students move on to the next proficiency levels, find new and better jobs, get their driver's license and most important of all, becoming U.S. Citizens after having passed all the requirements. Most of all, to say the least, I taught as Jesus did! I worked with the poorest of the poor in Indianapolis. While Americans enjoyed their vacations and other forms of entertainment, my students prepared food in restaurants and washed the dishes. They were the housekeepers who made our beds and cleaned our hotel rooms. These students had no friends but were right at home in my classroom, my classroom was a place to go to, a place to make new and long-lasting friendships. I taught my world of English language learners to live in harmony as they blended into American culture and the language spoken within this culture. I certainly had contributed to their livelihood. There was a real sense that I contributed meaningfully to their lives because I empowered my learners in the new language: to immerse themselves into American culture where this language is used, to further their education, make friends around the world, and participate in the global economy the best way they know-how. They have certainly used the global language I have taught them!

On-Going Retirement

When all the things you once did were managed easily and suddenly, these same responsibilities begin to take a toll on your stamina, it is time for retirement. Your body speaks to you and when that enthusiasm that awakened you to every new day does not present itself to you anymore, it is time to move on to a new direction in your life. There is a sense of obligation inviting you to a growing change! Once you are ready to take on retirement, you find yourself in a honeymoon stage, the thought of having more time to yourself, sleeping in, volunteering, going back home, and visiting places. While I am called to freedom and flexibility, I know it is necessary to have routines. There is an eventful urge to plan how I can be productive in my retirement. I am accustomed to combining spirituality, professionalism and domestic responsibility in my daily life.

Once long ago, I was on the treadmill of my career teaching full-time during the day and part-time in the evening. I taught English as a Second Language to speakers of other languages. I was always allowing myself to be challenged and this led me to a terribly busy life. Now, in retirement, I have slowed down, I take my time and I smell the roses along the way. There is no need to rush because I have so much time on my hands. How glorifying is that! I no longer see the need to work so hard or make a mark in my career. I still have a yearning desire to contribute to my favourite places through learning, giving, and receiving.

Currently, I work at a school cafeteria as a cafeteria assistant. I want to be in a school community because it is here where I am with children who keep me feeling young. After some soul searching, I saw the need to return to the very first place where I started my teaching career. I know that being in a Catholic school environment is so pleasing to my everyday life since it brings sweet memories of my first teaching days. Now, I do not have the responsibility of disciplining students, I just greet them every day with a smile as I take their orders and tell them to have a great lunch. I doubt if I ever wished my students many years ago to have a good lunch. I was too stressed out and just looked forward to having my own lunch period. Now is the time to make up those days. I am not obligated to be in school, I am there because I want to be involved in an important part of the students' day. It gives me this wonderful feeling that when I was a young teacher in the classroom, I assisted students with food for their minds and well-being. Today, in my senior years, I give them food to keep their bodies nourished. Prior to lunchtime, I prepare the lunch line, stocking it with all kinds of goodies that these young people will select for their trays. Working in the cafeteria is like Thanksgiving Day because of all the running around to get food ready, the washing of pots and pans, along with cleaning out the kitchen sinks for the next working day. I love to work in the kitchen for I have always been domestically inclined. I love the ladies who work with me, some are young mothers of the children who attend this school or grandmothers who choose to be around their grandchildren, while my manager is an experienced food handler of over twenty years throughout the diocese. I am neither a mother nor a grandmother, I have no children nor grandchildren, no dogs, nor cats. Perhaps, therefore, this is the right place for me. I chose to work in this happy place around children at the school cafeteria.

Of all other things, I like to do is sing and for this reason, I sing in my parish church choir. A member of the choir heard me singing in the congregation at one of the Marian services, so she invited me to join the choir. To this day, I will always be grateful that she invited me to sing. I consider choir practice which is held in the middle of the week my holy hour praising the Lord in song. On Sundays, I attend the 11:30 mass where I sing in the choir. My husband and I go to an earlier mass for our family time with God, so singing at the 11:30 mass is my time to entertain God in song and to cherish being with beautiful religious people with awesome singing voices. The Mass is a way of giving God His due. How wonderful it is to give God thanks at a second Sunday mass because Eucharist means thanksgiving. There is no greater way to show God how much I love Him after all He loved me first.

I also engage in another ministry, the Ministry of Hospitality. I greet people who come to mass, help with the Sunday collection and usher the line for Holy Communion. I love to give a friendly greeting to the people who come to church as I pass out the Sunday news bulletin after mass. How I enjoy thanking people for coming to worship and wishing them a good week. It is important to let the parishioners know that they are special people.

I also belong to the Good Samaritan group; our role is to assist in getting the meals ready for the grieving families immediately after the funerals. I enjoy this ministry because it reminds me of a tradition we have in Guam at all funerals. In Guam, there is a lot of feasting and celebrating of life by families, friends, and relatives who want to bring cheer to the grieving families.

I joined the GLYMERS group for it is so inspiring to meet others who have so gratefully and so happily advanced in years like me. We love being together, going to mass, having luncheon, then listening to guest speakers who assist us in redefining ourselves on our journey toward God at this life-changing time of our senior lives.

I also assist at weddings because I am a Wedding Assistant. How I love weddings for it reminds me of the movie, *The Sound of Music,* because I am genuinely like Maria in real life today. It is fascinating to be with people at the happiest moments of their lives. As the new couples make their marriage vows, I renew mine with a heart filled with gratitude for my own marriage.

I am in the Prayer Chain group in my parish. Every week, we receive a list of parishioners' families, relatives, and friends, or even yet of parishioners themselves who need prayers. Some are ill, some need help making tough decisions, and others need favours in their dilemmas, or need help with tough decisions. Our group's purpose is to petition God for His healing, love, mercy and compassion for them.

I volunteer to be a lector at Liturgical celebrations because I want to share the message and teachings of Christ through the readings. I want to grow spiritually by committing myself to the Proclamation of the Word to the congregation who are celebrating the Eucharist with me.

I also focus lots of attention on families. Whatever help I can provide for members of my family; I will be there to assist. I have no children, no grands, no dogs, nor cats. I invest my time and support to families who need my help under any circumstances since I am gifted with availability! Family is an extension of myself, it is my destiny to step forth when needed! I always believe that I can express my love for God in my eagerness to do good for them.

Since my father-in-law's death, I have engaged in visiting my mother-in-law twice a month. I just want to bring comfort to her and to see what kind of help she needs taken care of. My husband is like Mary in the Bible, he will sit and listen to mom as she talks and talks. I am like Martha who is in motion, cleaning toilet bowls and kitchen sinks, baking for her, or whatever else I see around her house that needs to be taken care of. To visit and provide help to someone who is grieving is a work of mercy and I like doing something beautiful for God.

I visited Fatima in Portugal, a beautiful site where one's devotion to the rosary is deepened. You marvel at the power of faith when you are there, and you embrace faith as a spiritual conviction that it is there to stay in your heart. This is the best place I have ever visited in my life, it being a very sacred site. I am so grateful to my brother who took me there and I am forever changed for having been there. Today, I cling to many rosaries daily, meditating on the life of Jesus and Mary and making them applicable to my life and the lives of those known to me near and far. I participate in the First Saturday rosary prayer group!

For my other retirement pastimes, I have many luncheon engagements with other retirees whom I have known over the years from the schools where I retired from, and from the church parish community that I attend today. I spend lots of time entertaining friends around my dinner table. I stay socially connected to keep healthy and happy. How I love to cook, bake, and entertain people in my home. Cooking and baking entertain me as I always love spending time in the kitchen.

I have travelled to Guam, Hawaii, and California to revisit my past with family and friends. In Guam, I reconnect with teacher friends who are also retired like me. We cherished talking about the good old teaching days and what some of our former students are doing with their lives today. We also reminisced about the many different activities we did as teachers for our students. Exchanging stories about all that is happening in our lives is such an awesome feeling. I have family members who are still living in Guam. All other relatives are invited to join us in our get-togethers feasting on the island's favourite delicacies that I have missed so much. Food prepared in coconut milk, beef and chicken marinated in vinegar, soy sauce, and onions, and freshly-barbecued fish soaked in soy sauce, fresh lemons, hot peppers, and green onions with cherry tomatoes. Such yummy foods! Food brings people together. In Guam you get invited to everybody's home, and you never have to worry about your next hot meal. In Hawaii, I have a niece and a nephew who stay on the military base with their families. It is advantageous to visit Hawaii when you have relatives there. They know where to go for the best local flavours of Hawaiian cuisine. We went to local restaurants instead of to tourist sites like those found in Waikiki since we do not want anything commercialised and crowded. The weather in Hawaii is fabulous and of course an island paradise for visitors like us. I found beautiful jewellery like Black Pearls and Corals in the shops there. In Hawaii, breakfast is served with brown rice with delicious Portuguese sausage, and spam prepared in all forms is also extremely popular. It was such a pleasant drive going around the island to see the black cliffs overlooking the seashore. Slow-moving rivers flow into the ocean and the islanders get on outrigger boats. Both Guam and Hawaii have the best beach destinations in the world where the sand is so white, and the water is so blue. They are known for their coral reefs, scuba diving, and surfing.

Other families live in Germany, Spain, and Hungary. Visiting these countries alerted me to so much cultural exchange. How captivating to be a part of their lifestyles and traditions as I was actively involved in what they did every day. Obviously, I was not a tourist since I got to visit the local people. Terraces of vineyards are common along the side of hills near every home in Germany. German homes are like chateaus staggered up on hills, built with three floors and most are multi-family homes. A typical German breakfast consists of hearty brot (breads) and Brotchen (rolls) decorated with butter, sweet jams and local honey, thinly sliced meats, cheese and even some Leberwurst. Main meals were served with wine every mid-day. We rode bikes to shop or to attend concerts in town. We hardly went anywhere by car for the fabulous trains took us to almost every destination.

Visited Budapest for a few days before heading to my sister in law's home.

Budapest is a huge city with very ancient buildings on the exterior, but their interiors are very modern, that it surprises you when you go inside. Hungarians live in exceedingly small ranch-type homes throughout the villages. Everybody has a garden filled with flowers, fruits or vegetables instead of yards Breakfast in Hungary is an open sandwich with fresh bread or toast, butter, cheese, different cream cheeses and topped with cold cuts, such as ham, bacon, salami, sausages such as beerwurst. The best version of Hungarian food is goulash. It is a slow-cooked beef with carrots, onions, and Hungary's trademark paprika to give it a kick. It is cooked over an open pit in a large pot for hours. All desserts are homemade and presented by the village women. My sister in law's brother owns a lovely cottage home right along the Danube River, we took a cruise on the Danube River. The city is spectacular at night, with lights illuminating Budapest's Chain Bridge, Parliament Building and other famous structures. The riverside is quite scenic, you become enchanted with the experience on a Danube River Cruise. Hungary is known for its hand-crafted porcelain, a homecoming gift which I received from my family and now graciously sits on my living room table.

In Spain, couples bring their children with them for happy hour and well into the night. This is considered family time! They do not have babysitters; the children play near them at the bar and grill restaurants while they socialise with friends over wine or beer. A must-try are Tapas which are small dishes typical for Spanish culture and are part of the social tradition of Spanish people. Tapas are designed to encourage conversation, so people are not so focused on eating an entire meal set before them. People from Spain party a lot and highlight their evenings with lots of fun conversation. When travelling in Northern Spain, you will not miss a typical building called horreos raised from the ground by pillars. They stand out as you enter any village because they are tiny unique huts raised on pillars with crosses on top of them. They are considered the unofficial symbol of Galicia in Northern Spain. Its original purpose was to store food for animals or to store any farm produce that needed to be stocked or further ripened. They are no longer utilised because of advancements in modern agriculture; however, they are still seen throughout Camino de Santiago because the people take pride in their farmland of many years ago.

I passed through mountainous Austria and Switzerland made brief stops and walked in many of their fascinating castles. They are perched on lofty hilltops and sometimes on riverbanks.

In the United States, I have visited New York, a metropolitan city in all its glow of cultural diversity. I visited Good Morning America and Kelly and Ryan studios in New York; I have been watching these morning shows from my living room every day for over twenty years. It was spectacular being right there. I visited the convent in North Carolina where I used to live, I had a good glimpse of it thirty years later. The Sisters I lived with back then have aged, but what remains are their voices. Their voices never changed! I may have forgotten them, but when they spoke, I remember who they were through their oral speech distinctive of them in my happy memories. They are my first family, my first friends!

I occasionally travel to Tampa our second home when my husband can have the weekends or holidays off. We always reconnect in our getaway home. We give so much time to biking the scenic trails throughout Tampa along magnificent waterways, lakefronts, or riverfronts. When I am home in Indianapolis, I do a lot of walking and biking on the Monon Trail across from our home. I find cleaning to be a valuable exercise for I accomplish two things while doing my daily chores, I engage in health and fitness, and I take pride in a refreshing home. Let me add, "Cleanliness is next to Godliness." I play Guam music every cleaning day. When my husband comes home from work, he knows that I am cleaning whenever he opens the door and hears Guam music playing. I sing a lot or listen to music to create sounds in the stillness of our beautiful home which has so much love in it.

Retirement is a golden time of my life where I can continue to pursue things that delight me, things I am passionate about. I am a simple woman with simple dreams. I take pleasure in small moments that most people take for granted or do not see. It is important to stay close to Him throughout your day whether you are running errands, doing chores, or just sitting. No moment is unimportant! I just do the ordinary things of life in an extraordinary way; this is how I find meaning and fulfilment. I marvel at the small things in life and I make them magnificent. I find friendship with God in everyday ways. I love making others happy because the joy I give them comes back to me. These are simple pleasures of life that money cannot buy. I smile at my world and my world smiles back at me. Faithfulness in the everyday moments of our lives prepares us for bigger things. I strive to live with this motto every day: Behold the handmaid of the Lord, be it done to me according to thy word. How pleased I am that I am named Mare!